BUILDING ON A DREAM

THE
SPACE
NEEDLE

Tamra B. Orr

PURPLE TOAD
PUBLISHING

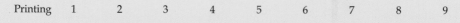

PURPLE TOAD
PUBLISHING

Printing   1   2   3   4   5   6   7   8   9

Big Ben
The Eiffel Tower
The Space Needle
The Statue of Liberty
The Sydney Opera House
The Taj Mahal

Publisher's Cataloging-in-Publication Data
Orr, Tamra.
The Space Needle / written by Tamra Orr.
    p. cm.
       Includes bibliographic references, glossary, and index.
ISBN 9781624692055
1. Space Needle (Seattle, Wash.)—Juvenile literature. 2. Architecture—Vocational guidance—Juvenile literature. I. Series: Building on a Dream.
    NA2555 2017
    507.8
                                    Library of Congress Control Number: 2016937176
eBook ISBN: 9781624692062

ABOUT THE AUTHOR: Tamra B. Orr is a full-time author living in the Pacific Northwest with her family. She is the author of more than 400 nonfiction books for readers of all ages. She is a graduate of Ball State University and spends a great deal of her free time reading and writing letters. Orr is lucky enough to live only a few hours from the Space Needle and has been there multiple times. It still astounds her.

CONTENTS

One of the biggest attractions to the World's Fair in Seattle was the new tall tower looming over the festival.

A Place to Celebrate

Helga Schmidt and Gene Shafer stood in line and tried to be patient. Like the thousands of other visitors to the 1962 Seattle World's Fair, they wanted to ride to the top of the brand-new Space Needle. The line for the elevator was long—and these two were nervous. They weren't afraid of heights or tired of standing in line. They were just eager to be married.

In late July, Helga, her parents, and Gene traveled to Oregon to visit his parents. Seattle was only a few hours away, so why not get married at the top of the Space Needle? Gene's father, who was a minister, could marry them. It would be a great memory! They got a marriage license, packed up both sets of future in-laws, and headed for Seattle. Now they were in line—and wishing it would go faster.

Their wish was granted. The news that they were going to be married when they got to the top had spread through the line. An employee overheard, and soon the wedding party was being escorted to the top of the tower. On July 27, Helga and Gene became the first couple to be married in the Space Needle.[1] They certainly were not the last. Today, many wedding planners help couples say "I do" hundreds of feet up in the air.

Other special events have occurred in the Space Needle. In 1974, a woman had a baby while visiting.[2] That same year, a deejay and his wife lived for six months in a small apartment on the observation deck.[3] From there, they broadcast their daily radio show. In 1975, two parachutists jumped from the top of the Needle—without permission.[4]

The following year, four more jumped, but this time it was part of a promotion for the Needle.

The Space Needle is one of the most unusual monuments in the United States. Unlike many other such buildings, it does not honor a famous person or moment in history. When it was built in 1962, it was meant to inspire people to think about the future. People were amazed by its alien and modern design. At more than 50 years old, the Needle still looks futuristic. Lit up in a darkening sky, it looks, for a moment, like a flying saucer hovering over the city.

In fact, some even suspected the Space Needle was built not to attract visitors from around the world, but from around the solar system! A group known as CHEESE (the Committee Hoping for Extra-Terrestrial Encounters to Save the Earth) was sure the Space Needle was a giant antenna.[5] They believed the government was using it to make contact with aliens. In 1978, Seattle hosted the second annual

Changing the lights and colors of the Space Needle is one way Seattle celebrates holidays and other events.

On New Year's Eve an entirely different kind of light takes over at the Space Needle. Fireworks are set off from the top of the tower, filling the sky with bright colors and flashes.

science-fiction exposition. The management of the Space Needle wanted to play a part in the event, so special lights were added to make the building look like an actual spaceship floating in the night sky.

CHEESE was right about one thing—the Space Needle does have an antenna on top. It doubles as an aircraft beacon, warning low-flying planes away from it. In 2005, it became a Wi-Fi antenna for the people of the city. A camera is mounted on the spire of the Space Needle. Its videos are often featured on the nightly news.

The Seattle Space Needle is a beautiful sight on the city's skyline. How did such an incredible building get built—and why?

It all began with a satellite called *Sputnik*.

When the Russians launched *Sputnik* in late 1957, it began the world's fascination with exploring space. A few months later, NASA launched its first satellite, *Explorer 1*.

Space Cage on a Napkin

In 1957, Russia shocked the world—and it changed the United States in countless ways.

On October 4, Russia rocketed the first man-made satellite into space. Called *Sputnik*, it was the size of a basketball and weighed only about 180 pounds. It traveled 500 miles above the Earth, orbiting the planet every 98 minutes.[1] It was a huge achievement for Russia and for space exploration. It also terrified the United States. At the time, Russia and the United States were involved in a cold war. While there were no actual battles, the two countries were not on friendly terms. The idea that the "enemy" had this much technology created panic. What if Russia was developing missiles? Would it attack America?

The launching of *Sputnik* spurred a "space race." The United States put its focus—and a lot of money—on catching up with Russia's space program. By early 1958, the United States sent up its own satellite, *Explorer 1*. On July 29 that year, the government created the National Aeronautics and Space Administration, better known as NASA.[2] Everywhere people turned, from the news to the classroom, from politicians to librarians, space was the number one topic.

While the push for space exploration was happening, many of the powerful people in Seattle were thinking about the upcoming 1962 World's Fair. It would be a chance to show off their city to the entire world. What could they do to really wow visitors? What could they build that would be like nothing else in the country?

Carlson and Senator Warren Magnuson examine a model of the Space Needle. Choosing the right shape was as challenging as finding the money to build it.

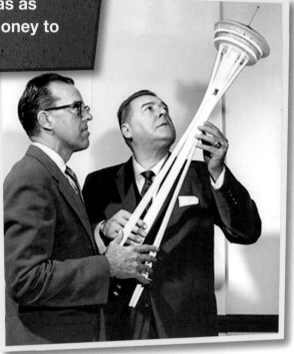

These were the questions Edward Carlson, president of Western International Hotels, was asking one afternoon in 1959. He had been chosen as the chairman of the upcoming World's Fair. In the spring while he was visiting Germany, he was invited to have dinner at the Stuttgart Tower. It was a tall, cylindrical tower with a restaurant at the top. Fast elevators zoomed diners upward, and the ride had thrilled the chairman. Was this the idea he had been looking for?

Carlson pulled out a napkin and sketched his idea for a tall tower, including a restaurant at the top. Could this work in Seattle? Visitors would be able to see incredible views from the top, from Puget Sound to the nearby peaks of Mount Baker, Mount Rainier, and even as far away as Mount St. Helens. But wait! Could the top of the tower look a bit like a spaceship? It might inspire more visitors to come to the fair, and it would certainly tap into the country's passion for space travel.

Carlson sent his drawing to Jack Graham, the architect hired for the project. Graham was intrigued. When his business partner, Jim Jackson, suggested that the restaurant at the top *revolve*, everyone was excited.[3] There were only a few other revolving restaurants in the entire world. How could they build it? Would it turn on tracks? Would it need gears? Would it be smooth enough that people could still eat and drink without spilling anything? Graham was sure it could be done.

The design for the Space Needle—originally named the Space Cage—changed many times. In one design, the tower looked more like a hot-air balloon than a flying saucer. Then the partners spent weeks trying to figure out how to support the saucer. One column? Multiple legs? Finally, they chose a three-legged design. Originally, they planned to make the legs out of concrete. They ended up using steel, as it was stronger and more durable.

By fall 1960, the plans for the Space Needle were finally approved. Since the World's Fair was set to open in 18 months, they didn't have much time. It seemed like an impossible task—especially since no land had been chosen yet to build it on. Where would it go? Once a site was located, could the construction be completed in time for the fair? And who would pay for the project? These were difficult questions—but the answers were just around the corner.

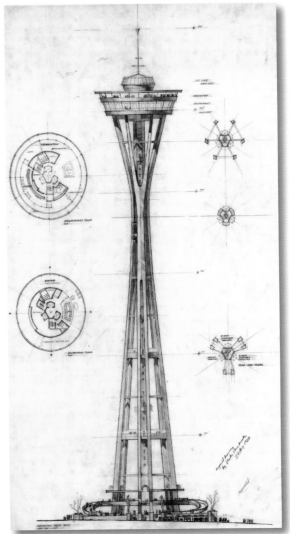

An early design for the Space Needle

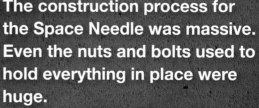

The construction process for the Space Needle was massive. Even the nuts and bolts used to hold everything in place were huge.

"The 400-Day Wonder"

The search for a place to build the Space Needle was a desperate one. The land had to be located somewhere on the fairgrounds, and it had to be big enough to support the tower. Most of the land was already owned. Days passed. Weeks passed. Finally, they found an old fire station that had been turned into a fire alarm office. The plot it was on measured 120 feet by 120 feet—just big enough. The fair was only 13 months away, so time was short.

As one Space Needle team searched for the right piece of land, another team worked to secure the money to build the monument. The funding team had to convince business owners that the Space Needle and its restaurant would earn profits. Finally, many business owners were willing to invest in it.

At last, on April 17, 1961, the first shovel of dirt was dug at the site. Bulldozers continued to dig. In 11 days, there was a hole 30 feet deep and 120 feet square.[1]

On May 26, 467 trucks took turns pouring cement into the hole in the ground. In less than 12 hours, the hole was filled. More than 50 years later, the record still stood: This was the largest, nonstop concrete pour in the western United States. The total weight of the foundation was an astonishing 5,850 tons, including 250 tons of rebar. The foundation weighed far more than the Space Needle itself.[2]

Once the foundation was complete, it was time to start building the Space Needle's three supporting legs. They would be anchored into the foundation with 72 four-inch bolts, each one 30-feet long.[3] Finding a way to make the steel bend and curve as the legs reached up

As the Space Needle grew taller, the crane grew larger, moving up higher and higher above the ground.

to support the restaurant was difficult. Workers had to use welding torches to heat the metal enough to shape it.

A special crane was built to fit inside the Space Needle's central tower. As the work progressed, the crane went higher and higher in the tower.

By September 1, the tower was 200 feet tall. Wet weather was on its way, and the rush was on to get the tower finished before the fair opened in April.

The weeks passed, and slowly the Space Needle grew. In order to support the restaurant, a 20-ton ring of steel had to be raised hundreds of feet into the air. In addition to building the restaurant, construction workers also built offices, restrooms, a kitchen, and a gift shop. The diameter of the restaurant was 94.5 feet. The diameter of the halo around it was 138 feet.[4] Two observation decks were added for people to see unforgettable views of Seattle.

The Space Needle was built to withstand a 7.8-magnitude earthquake and up to 200-mile-per-hour winds. On windy days the tower sways. In fact, it moves about an inch for every 10 miles per hour that the wind blows.[5]

Workers were startled to find that the crane they had been relying on could not reach the halo at the top of the Space Needle. How would the louvers on the halo be installed without the crane? Very brave workers crawled out on six-inch-wide strips of steel, 515 feet above the ground, and bolted them into place.

The last piece to be installed was a torch that was 50 feet tall. It burned throughout the duration of the fair, using enough natural gas to heat 125 homes. After the fair, the torch was never used again. A total of 24 lightning rods (not counting the spire) were added to the top of the Needle. They would protect the tower by directing lightning strikes to the ground.[6]

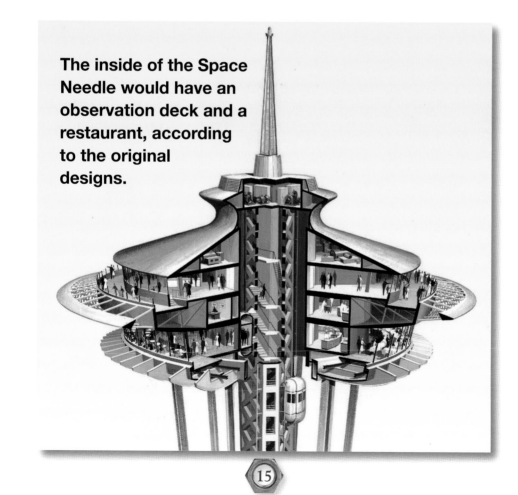

The inside of the Space Needle would have an observation deck and a restaurant, according to the original designs.

The architects had hoped to include a stork's nest at the top of the Needle, but the idea was scrapped. They realized that storks only live in warmer climates. They were not likely to stick around in Seattle's chilly temperatures, and would simply fly away when cold weather came.[7]

Getting the 42-ton crane back down through the central tower was a nightmare. It had to be moved very slowly, and it took every single construction worker's help to make sure it was done safely. Finally, on December 20, 1961, the crane was back on the ground.

Once the framework was done, elevators were installed to rush people from the base to the top. This job came down to the last minute—the final elevator arrived the day before the World's Fair opened! Each of these special elevators can carry 25 people and is connected by seven cables. Each has a brake that engages if the elevator starts to drop too fast. Two of the elevators are high speed, traveling at 10 miles per hour. That is 800 feet per

Each elevator has seven cables. Each cable is strong enough to hold the elevator by itself.

minute, so it takes only 43 seconds to go from the bottom to the top. When it is snowing, people are shocked when they look through the glass elevator windows. The snow appears to go up instead of down. Snowflakes travel 3 miles per hour, slower than the elevators. They appear to "fall up" as the elevator goes down.[8]

The last few months were busy. Appliances, furniture, and heating and air-conditioning systems were installed. Painting and other finishing touches were done. At last, the "The 400-Day Wonder" was ready to amaze everyone at America's Space Age World's Fair.

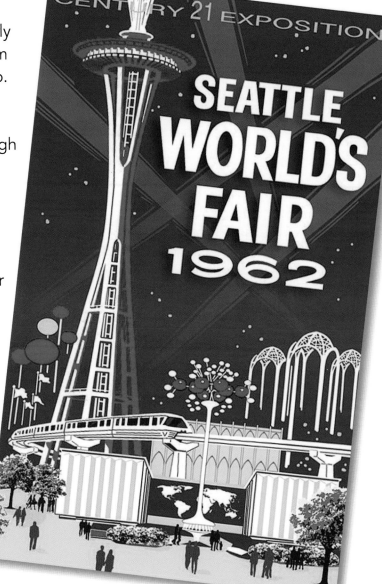

The Space Needle was finished just in time for people to walk through the gates of the World's Fair.

The focus of the World's Fair was the world of tomorrow. Visitors rode the futuristic-looking monorail, looked at science-fiction styled cars, and took a ride in the space-age "Bubbleator" elevator.

Welcome to the World's Fair!

News of the World's Fair in Seattle spread all across the world. Dozens of countries set up exhibits at the fair. The February 1962 issue of *Holiday* magazine invited everyone to head to the Pacific Northwest city to see the Century 21 Exposition:

> Look at cities in the year 2000, see homes whose walls are jets of air, where cordless appliances work for you, cars ride without wheels, TV wrist telephones speed everyday communications . . . You will soar past the moon into outer galaxies—no space suit, no gravity, in the $9 million complex of the United State Science Pavilion. ... But it's not all about the story of man's great tomorrows. Much of this $80 million show will be a glittering world of today. Dine atop the towering 60-story Space Needle which revolves to view Mt. Rainier . . . [1]

The World's Fair drew millions of people to Seattle. On opening day, more than 500 bells rang, 2,000 balloons were released, and 10 Air Force F-102 fighter jets roared overhead. People came to see the exhibits and displays, and also to listen to musicians and watch other performers. They took rides on the city's futuristic-feeling monorail. By the time the fair ended six months later, 9.6 million people had visited.[2]

Of those millions, many flocked directly to the Space Needle. An astounding 20,000 people paid to ride the elevators up to the observation decks *every single day* of the fair. A total of 2.75 million

The SkyCity restaurant

people had ridden the elevators by the time the fair ended.[3] Many of them also stopped to eat in the revolving restaurant, The Eye of the Needle. (The restaurant is now called SkyCity.)

The revolving restaurant is a fascinating place to eat. The outer 14 feet of the floor turns, while the center does not. The part that turns does so very slowly. In fact, it takes almost an hour (58 minutes) to make an entire revolution. It runs on tracks, and a simple 1.5 horsepower electric motor keeps it going. That is the same size motor found in many vacuum cleaners![4]

The servers struggle at first to remember which table ordered what food because, by the time the order is ready to serve, the table has moved from where it was before. Many people order the Lunar Orbiter, a sundae served over a dish of dry ice. It looks like it is steaming, and is presented as if coming in for a landing. Ice cream is combined with syrup and fruit. This dessert has been served since opening day.

The Space Needle has been painted many colors. During the World's Fair, it had white legs, an olive green core, a gold roof, and red louvers. It took more than 1,340 gallons to paint it from top to bottom. In 1968, it was painted all white and gold. Since then it has been painted many times, using 2,000 gallons of paint each time. The top of the Needle is often painted to support local sports teams. It has featured the logo of the University of Washington Huskies football team, the Seattle Mariners, and the Seattle SuperSonics.[5]

Many changes have happened inside as well. In 1982, the SkyLine banquet hall was added at 100 feet. Another pavilion was also added.[6] In 1993, the elevators were replaced. In 1999, the City's Landmarks Preservation Board named the Space Needle an official City of Seattle Landmark. The board stated, "The Space Needle marks a point in history of the City of Seattle and represents American aspirations towards technological prowess. [It] embodies in its form and construction the era's belief in commerce, technology, and progress."[7]

The following year, a new entrance, fountain, and gift shop were built. The renovations cost more than $20 million—more than four times what it cost to build the entire monument in 1962.

More than one million people visit the Space Needle each year. More than 50 years after it was built, it is still considered the number one tourist attraction in the Pacific Northwest.

The entrance to the Space Needle

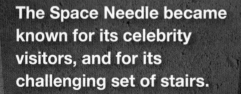

The Space Needle became known for its celebrity visitors, and for its challenging set of stairs.

CHAPTER 5

On the Screen—and into the Future!

Even people who have not been able to visit the Space Needle in person have most likely seen it on the screen. Over the years, the monument has appeared in a number of television shows and movies.

During the World's Fair, Elvis Presley came to Seattle to film *It Happened at the World's Fair*. Other films featuring the Space Needle include *The Parallax View* (1974), *Sleepless in Seattle* (1993), *Austin Powers: The Spy Who Shagged Me* (1999), and *Chronicle* (2012).

Several television shows have also used the Space Needle as a backdrop, including *Frasier*, *Dark Angel*, *Grey's Anatomy*, and *iCarly*. In 2012, the Seattle monument even hosted the first challenge of season 10 of *Top Chef*. Many celebrities have traveled to the top of the Needle, including Demi Moore, John Travolta, Tim Robbins, Scott Bakula, and Bruce Lee. Famous athletes and musicians, as well as presidents and other world leaders, have visited the Space Needle. Macklemore & Ryan Lewis ended their "Can't Hold Us" video with Macklemore hoisting a flag on the Space Needle's spire.

The Space Needle has won many awards. It is repeatedly voted the Best Restaurant with a View. It has also been named the best place to get engaged, get married, or have a party.

In 2015, the public was allowed to climb the Needle's open-air staircases. As part of the Base 2 Space stair climb, participants would climb the 848 steps that go from the ground to the observation deck, 520 feet up. The money they raised would go to the Fred Hutchinson Cancer Research Center.[1]

While most visitors to the Space Needle are thrilled with the view from the restaurant or observation deck, some daring people would like to see even more. They wish they could walk out to the edge of the halo surrounding the observation deck. Some even want to climb all the way out to the spire, which is 605 feet above the ground. Clearly these feats would be very dangerous, but there may be a safe way for them to have the experience.

The Space Needle is working on a cell phone application that will allow people to virtually stand on top of the monument or even fly around it using virtual reality headsets. For those who want to see the view from the comfort of home, a webcam shows a view of Seattle around the clock.[2]

When Edward Carlson first drew a tall tower on his napkin that day in Germany, he most likely could not have imagined that half a century later his idea would still be drawing people to Seattle year round. The futuristic saucer still grabs people's attention. It reminds them how determination, creativity, and dedication can turn a dream into solid reality.

Carlson's "dream"

The Space
Needle glows
over Seattle.

Number of Windows around the Top: 48

Total Weight: 9,550 tons

The center of gravity for the Space Needle is 5 feet above the ground.

The SkyLine level, at 100 feet, was built in 1982.

The Legacy Light, or SkyBeam, has three 7-kilowatt spotlights with the combined power of 85 million candles.

The camera mounted on the spire is called the PanoCam. It shows views of Seattle through its web site, http://www.spaceneedle.com/webcam/

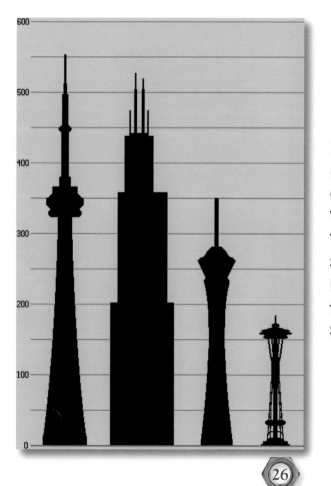

Height in meters (left to right): CN Tower, Toronto; Willis Tower (Sears Tower), Chicago; Stratosphere, Las Vegas; the Space Needle, Seattle

1957 October 4: Russia launches *Sputnik*.

1958 The United States sends up *Explorer 1*; the U.S. government creates NASA.

1959 Edward Carlson visits Stuttgart, Germany, and is inspired by the Stuttgart Tower.

1960 Plans for the Space Needle are approved.

1961 April 7: The first shovel of dirt is dug at the site for the Space Needle.

May 26: Cement trucks pour the foundation nonstop for 12 hours.

September 1: The Space Needle reaches 200 feet.

December 20: The crane is brought back down to the ground.

1962 April 21: The Seattle World's Fair officially opens. It is also called the Century 21 Exposition.

July 27: The first wedding is held at the Space Needle.

October 21: The Seattle World's Fair officially closes.

1968 The Space Needle is painted white and gold.

1974 A baby is born at the Space Needle.

1975 Parachutists jump from the Space Needle.

1982 The annual New Year's Eve fireworks show begins at the Needle. Massive renovations begin.

1993 All the elevators are replaced.

1999 The Space Needle is named an official City of Seattle landmark.

2011 The Legacy Light on top of the Space Needle shines for 11 days straight after the September 11 terrorist attacks on New York City and Washington, D.C.

2015 The first Base 2 Space fundraising event is held.

Chapter 1

1. "Needle Is Wedding Site," *Spokane Daily Chronicle,* July 28, 1962. https://news.google.com/newspapers?nid=1338&dat=19620728&id=xq9 YAAAAIBAJ&sjid=ZPcDAAAAIBAJ&pg=4968,6626327&hl=en
2. "Baby Born on Space Needle," *The Bulletin,* June 11, 1974. https://news. google.com/newspapers?nid=1243&dat=19740611&id=Ngg0AAAAIBAJ &sjid=HvgDAAAAIBAJ&pg=2617,6657941&hl=en
3. "Space Needle 50th Anniversary," *SpaceNeedle50.com.* http://www. spaceneedle50.com/1970s.aspx
4. Michael Arbeiter, "15 Things You Might Not Know about the Space Needle," *Mental Floss,* http://mentalfloss.com/article/66548/15-things-you-might-not-know-about-space-needle
5. "Space Needle Facts." Facts.net http://facts.net/space-needle-facts/

Chapter 2

1. Danielle Burton, "10 Things You Didn't Know about Sputnik." *US News and World Report.* September 28, 2007. http://www.usnews.com/news/world/articles/2007/09/28/10-things-you-didnt-know-about-sputnik
2. Ibid.
3. Chelsea Gurrow, "The Space Needle and the World's Fair of 1962; 'The Biggest Thing since Lewis and Clark.'" *OPB.* June 30, 2013. http://www. opb.org/news/article/the-space-needle-and-the-worlds-fair-of-1962-the-biggest-thing-since-lewis-and-clark/

Chapter 3

1. "Space Needle: The Structure," *Space Needle.* http://www.spaceneedle. com/fun-facts/
2. Ibid.
3. Ibid.

4. Ibid.

5. Ibid.

6. Seattle Magazine Staff, "Space Needle Trivia," *Seattle Magazine*, February 2012. http://www.seattlemag.com/article/space-needle-trivia

7. "Space Needle: The Structure."

8. Ibid.

Chapter 4

1. Matt Novak, "Construction Begins on the Space Needle (1961)," *Paleofuture*, April 17, 2011. http://paleofuture.com/blog/2011/4/17/construction-begins-on-thespace-needle-1961-512626001

2. Ibid.

3. "Century 21 World's Fair," Seattle Municipal Archives. Economic Research Associates preliminary findings on 1962 World's Fair attendance and capacity, April 12, 1962. Folder 11, Box 196, Wesley C. Uhlman Subject Files, 5287-02. Seattle Municipal. http://www.seattle.gov/Documents/Departments/CityArchive/DDL/WorldsFair/Apr121962.pdf

4. "Space Needle: The Structure."

5. Arbeiter.

6. "Space Needle: The Structure."

7. Ibid.

Chapter 5

1. "Base 2 Space FAQ," Space Needle. http://www.spaceneedle.com/b2s-faq/

2. Matt Matovich, "Want to Stand on Top of the Space Needle? There's an App for That," KOMONews.com, April 22, 2015. http://www.komonews.com/news/local/Want-to-stand-on-the-top-of-the-Space-Needle-Theres-an-app-forthat-301012651.html

Works Consulted

"10.3.15: Base 2 Space—Seattle's Most Iconic Climb" May 8, 2015, *Space Needle News.* http://www.spaceneedle.com/news/2015/05/base-2-space/

Burton, Danielle. "10 Things You Didn't Know About *Sputnik.*" *U.S. News & World Report,* September 28, 2007. http://www.usnews.com/news/world/articles/2007/09/28/10-things-you-didnt-know-about-Sputnik

"Century 21 World's Fair." Seattle.gov, undated. http://www.seattle.gov/cityarchives/exhibits-and-education/digital-document-libraries/century-21-worlds-fair

Doherty, Craig A. *The Seattle Space Needle.* Woodbridge, CT: Blackbirch Press, 1997.

Hodson, Jeff. "Sky Beams on Space Needle Will Glow for New Years's Eve." *Seattle Times,* December 16, 1999. http://community.seattletimes.nwsource.com/archive/?date=19991216&slug=3001814

Mansfield, Harold. *The Space Needle Story.* Mercer Island, WA: Writing Works, Inc., 1962.

Matovich, Matt. "Want to Stand on Top of the Space Needle? There's an App for That." KOMONews.com, April 22, 2015. http://www.komonews.com/news/local/Want-to-stand-on-the-top-of-the-Space-Needle-Theres-an-app-for-that-301012651.html

Novak, Matt. "Construction Begins on the Space Needle (1961)." *Paleofuture,* April 17, 2011. http://paleofuture.com/blog/2011/4/17/construction-begins-on-the-space-needle-1961.html

Seattle Magazine Staff. "Space Needle Trivia!" *Seattle Magazine,* February 2012. http://www.seattlemag.com/article/space-needle-trivia

Spector, Robert. *The Space Needle: Symbol of Seattle.* Seattle, WA: Documentary Media LLC, 2002.

On the Internet

Seattle Space Needle Official Site http://www.spaceneedle.com/home/

World Federation of Great Towers: Space Needle. Undated. http://www.great-towers.com/towers/space-needle/

architect (AR-kih-tekt)—A person who designs buildings and other construction.

beacon (BEE-kun)—A guiding or warning signal.

cold war—A struggle over different ideas carried on by methods other than physical fighting.

cylindrical (sil-IN-drih-kul)—Having the shape of a cylinder, like a can.

exposition (eks-poh-ZIH-shun)—A public event or show of technology or industrial products.

extra-terrestrial (EKS-trah-tuh-RES-tree-ul)—From outside the limits of the earth; from space.

logo (LOH-goh)—A symbol of an organization, such as a business or a sports team.

louver (LOO-ver)—One of a set of narrow openings for admitting light and air.

orbit (OR-bit)—The curved path around a planet; to travel along this path.

pavilion (puh-VIL-yun)—An open tent or airy building used for concerts and exhibits.

prowess (PROW-ess)—Great skill.

rebar (REE-bar)—Steel rods used to strengthen concrete.

renovation (reh-noh-VAY-shun)—An improvement or change.

satellite (SAH-tuh-lyt)—A natural body or a human-made object that orbits a planet.

virtual (VER-choo-ul)—Existing only online or in the imagination.

PHOTO CREDITS: p. 3—Kathy Haven; p. 7—Shannon Kringen; p. 8—Rostlina; p. 12—Bennacche; p. 16—Just Julie; p. 18—Seattle Municipal Archives, JMabel; Larry Cragin; p. 22—Deano, David. All other photos—Creative Commons. Every measure has been taken to find all copyright holders of material used in this book. In the event any mistakes or omissions have happened within, attempts to correct them will be made in future editions of the book.